Angel Ivy

Michael Trillow

In loving memory of our daughter Ivy, who continues to be a part of our family every day.

www.ivysgifts.co.uk
www.thepoeticparent.co.uk

Angel Ivy

Michael Trillow

My name is Angel Ivy
And I just came by to say,
That I'm here to look after you
Each and every day.

You see, I'm kind of magic
Because you can't see me there.
But know I'm never far away
Showing just how much I care.

I like to send you messages,
Like a buzzing bumblebee,

I try to tell you that I love you
But you can't hear, "Oops!" I forgot,
I can only talk in whispers
But I can hear an awful lot.

So talk and I will listen
And I'll try to help you out,
It may take a little while though
As I might not be about.

Some days I might be busy,
There is so much here to do,
So talk with Mummy and Daddy
As they can help you too.

I have a very tricky job
So could you lend a hand?
Because when we work together
We're the best team in the land.

Being kind and helping others
Helps them to have nice days,
It also makes you feel good
In a lot of different ways.

Saying please and thank you
Shows that you're polite,
Then people will all smile at you
Because you say things right.

If you ever really need me,
Even if you just want to play,
Remember I am always around,
I am just a thought away.

Sometimes if I cuddle you,
You may feel a little cold.

Mummy and Daddy have a saying
"Forever loved, always together"
So know that I am with you
And I won't leave you ever.

Printed in Great Britain
by Amazon